HOW-TO LIBRARY

MAKING A PAPER AIRPLANE
AND OTHER PAPER TOYS

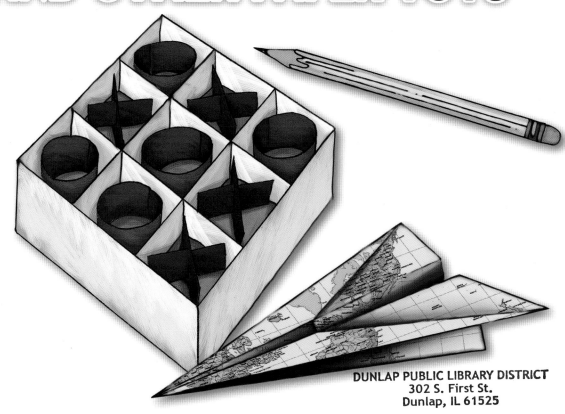

By Dana Meachen Rau • Illustrated by Kathleen Petelinsek

CHERRY LAKE PUBLISHING • ANN ARBOR, MICHIGAN

CHERRY LAKE
Publishing

A NOTE TO ADULTS:
Please review the instructions for these craft projects before your children make them. Be sure to help them with any crafts you do not think they can safely conduct on their own.

A NOTE TO KIDS:
Be sure to ask an adult for help with these craft activities when you need it. Always put your safety first!

Published in the United States of America by Cherry Lake Publishing
Ann Arbor, Michigan
www.cherrylakepublishing.com

Content Adviser: Dr. Julia L. Hovanec, Professor of Art Education, Kutztown University, Kutztown, Pennsylvania

Photo Credits: Page 4, ©Lena Sergeeva/Shutterstock, Inc.; page 5, ©iStockphoto.com/kate_sept2004; page 6, ©Kamira/Shutterstock, Inc.; page 7, ©Olga Kovalenko/Shutterstock, Inc.; page 29, ©Dleonis/Dreamstime.com; page 32, ©Tania McNaboe

Library of Congress Cataloging-in-Publication Data
Rau, Dana Meachen, 1971–
Making a paper airplane and other paper toys/by Dana Meachen Rau.
p. cm.—(How-to library. Crafts)
Includes bibliographical references and index.
ISBN 978-1-61080-473-8 (lib. bdg.) —
ISBN 978-1-61080-560-5 (e-book) — ISBN 978-1-61080-647-3 (pbk.)
1. Paper airplanes—Juvenile literature. 2. Paper toys—Juvenile literature.
I. Title.
 TL778.R38 2012
745.592—dc23   2012005508

Cherry Lake Publishing would like to acknowledge the work of The Partnership for 21st Century Skills. Please visit www.21stcenturyskills.org for more information.

Printed in the United States of America
Corporate Graphics Inc.
July 2012
CLFA11

*The author would like to thank Michelle Hawran
for her piñata-making enthusiasm and expertise.*

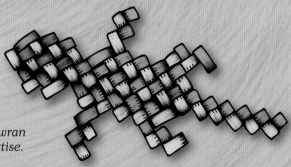

TABLE OF CONTENTS

Homemade Paper Toys

Rainy day? Have fun indoors instead!

Have you ever been stuck indoors on a rainy day? How do you pass the time? Do you watch television? Read a book? Clean your room? You may have bins and shelves filled with toys and games. They can keep you busy for hours.

A piece of paper can keep you busy, too. Paper is not just for writing. You can **transform** paper into unique toys to play with, display, and share with friends. You don't even need expensive craft supplies. You may have most of the tools you need right at home.

Think of some of your favorite toys and games. Then think of ways you could make your own version of them. Maybe you can invent a board game. Make a zoo of paper animals. Turn a flat piece of paper into a **three-dimensional** sculpture.

You'll discover that homemade toys and games can be more fun than ones that come from a store!

Think of all the things you can make with paper.

Before and After Paper

Ancient people carved pictures into stone.

Ancient people recorded information and made art just as we do today. But they didn't use paper. They carved images and words on stone **tablets** or pieces of wood. They also painted on fabric. The ancient Chinese were the first to make paper, in about 105 CE. Their idea soon spread to many other cultures.

People used paper to record important information. It also became an important **medium** for artists. People could draw and paint on it. They could mix and layer it with glue to make solid objects. They could fold it into different forms.

Origami is an important Japanese tradition. Origami artists transform single squares of paper into the shapes of animals and other objects without cutting or using glue. After Arabs brought paper to Spain in the 1100s, the Spanish developed a similar paper folding art called papiroflexia.

You can create art with paper, too. Fold it into interesting shapes. Mold it onto forms with paste. Link it together in a colorful chain. You can even make paper fly.

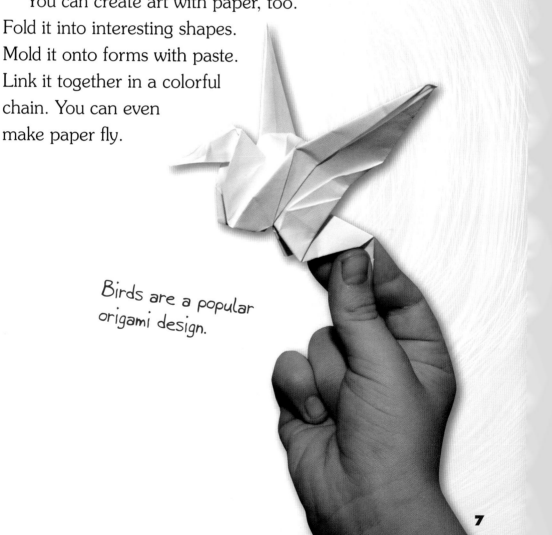

Birds are a popular origami design.

Basic Tools

Take a trip to the art, hobby, or scrapbooking store. You'll find whole aisles stocked with paper. Paper comes in all different colors, designs, and **textures**. These are some of your choices:

- Copy paper is used in copy machines and printers.
- Decorative paper is decorated with patterns and colors.
- Card stock is thicker paper used to make cards.
- Tissue paper is very thin paper.
- Newsprint is the type used for newspapers.
- Origami paper is small square paper.
- Mat board is very thick board used for making sturdy creations.

Check out your trash, too! Paper that you might normally throw away can be used for projects. Used magazines, calendars, wrapping paper, cereal boxes, or greeting cards may have interesting patterns or images you could use. Paint sample chips from the hardware store come in a wide range of colors. Keep a drawer or bin of interesting paper scraps so you have little bits whenever you need them.

Decorative paper comes in many colors.

Some other tools you might use for paper projects include:

- Cutting tools, such as scissors, a craft knife, or a paper cutter
- Adhesives, such as white glue, clear tape, double-sided tape, or duct tape
- Decorating supplies, such as markers, paint, crayons, or stickers
- A ruler for measuring and making straight lines
- A pencil for marking measurements and drawing lines

SHARP TOOL SAFETY
Cutting tools are very sharp. Prot
yourself. Always ask for an adult
assistance when using these
tools. Protect your work surface
by placing a thick mat, piece of
cardboard, or wooden board under
your paper when you cut.

Gather together all the materials you will need for your project.

Crisp Creases

When making paper
projects, it is important
to make sure your
measurements are exact
and your **creases** are straight and crisp.

Measuring

- Use a ruler with easy-to-read numbers.
- Mark measurements and draw lines using a sharp pencil.
- Check and double-check your measurements.

Creasing

- Fold your paper on a flat surface.
- Line up corners and edges well.
- Press down the center of the fold with your finger.
  Then run the side of your fingernail back
  and forth across the crease so
  it lies completely flat.

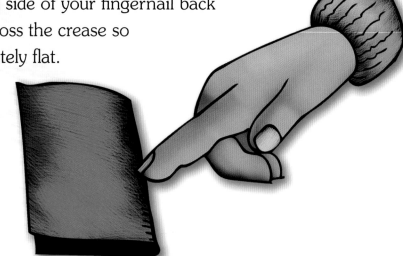

Crease your
paper so it will
stay where you
want it.

Scoring

For thicker paper, it helps to **score** your line before you fold. Scoring cuts through the top layer of the paper without cutting all the way through.

- Place your ruler along your fold line.
- With one tip of the scissors, gently trace along the line while pulling toward the ruler. Be careful not to cut through the paper.
- Fold the paper away from you along the line.

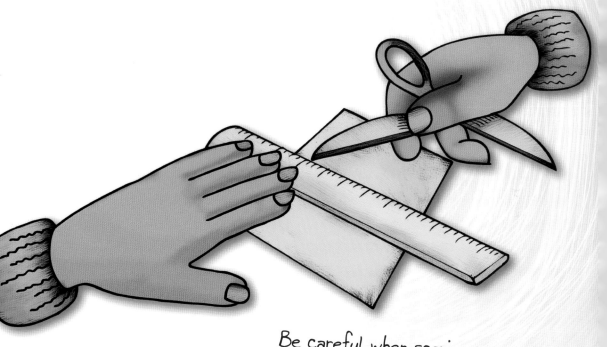

Be careful when scoring a line. Hold the ruler with one hand and the scissors with the other.

Types of Folds

You can make many projects with just a few simple folds.

Valley Fold

A valley fold is shown in directions with a dashed line. Fold the paper in half by bringing one edge to the other in front. The paper makes a V, or valley shape.

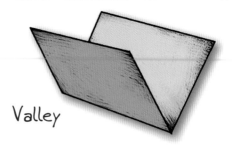

Valley

Mountain Fold

A mountain fold is shown in directions with a dotted and dashed line. Fold the paper in half by bringing one edge to the other in back. The paper makes a pointed mountain shape.

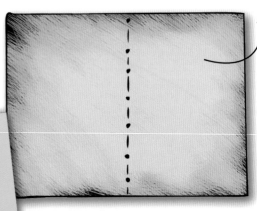

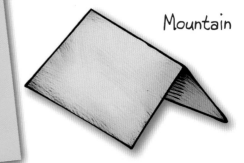

Mountain

EASY INSTRUCTIONS
Paper folding became a popular craft worldwide thanks to a man named Akira Yoshizawa. In the mid-1900s, he created standard symbols for origami instructions. This helped make it easier for people to follow directions.

Accordion Fold

An accordion fold is a combination of mountain and valley folds. Folding in one direction and then the other makes a zigzag shape.

First fold the bottom edge of the paper in a valley fold. Then fold the edge back into a mountain fold. Repeat until you have reached the top of the paper.

Accordian

Folding Symbols

Folding directions often use symbols. Here are a few you should know:

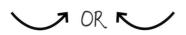 OR

This arrow means fold toward you.

OR

This arrow means fold away from you.

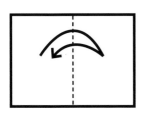

This arrow means fold, crease, and unfold again.

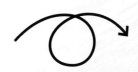

This arrow means turn the project over.

Stand Up with Slots

You can cut slots into pieces of paper and slip them onto each other. This can help you make projects that stand up.

Here's how to make paper stand up with slots:

1. Cut two pieces of thick paper (such as card stock or cardboard) the same size.
2. With a ruler, find the center of each paper and mark it with a pencil dot.
3. Use scissors to cut a slot from the edge to the center on each piece of paper.
4. Slide one slot into the other. Your papers will stand up.

Make sure your slots go to the exact center of the paper.

Experiment with slots to figure out other shapes you can build. For the best fit, cut your lines straight and try not to cut past the center point.

Slots are useful for building many kinds of paper shapes.

Indoor Snowballs

Make snowballs in the middle of summer! Toss these softer snowballs indoors when you're in the mood for a harmless snowball fight.

Materials

2 two-ply white tissues
String or thread
Scissors

You can make these snowballs on even the hottest days.

Steps

1. Lay one tissue on top of the other. You will have four layers of tissue in all.
2. Fold up the bottom edge about 1 inch (2.5 centimeters). Continue folding the tissue in a 1-inch accordion fold up to the top.
3. Fold the strip of tissue in half. Tie a piece of string in the center.
4. Use scissors to cut the folded end.
5. Fan out the tissues on each side of the center string. Very gently, start pulling apart the four layers of tissue.
6. Continue separating the tissue all the way around until you have a soft snowball.

COLORFUL POM-POMS
You can also use tissue p[aper] for this project if you don['t] have tissues on hand. Cut [?] pieces about 8 x 8 inches (20 x 20 cm) and layer the[m] on top of each other. Use a variety of colors to make pom-poms that you can toss around at a birthday party.

Zoom the Room Airplane

Are you ready to see the world—
or maybe just zoom across the family room? Make a paper
airplane out of an old map, and test how far and high it can fly.

Materials

An old map, cut to 8½ x 11 inches
(21.6 x 28 cm) (If you don't have an
old map, regular paper will also work.)
Clear tape

Start by creasing and unfolding your sheet of paper.

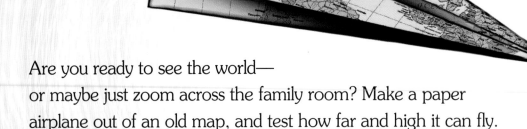

Steps

1. Fold the paper or map in
   half lengthwise. Crease.
   Unfold.
2. Fold in the two top corners
   to the center crease.

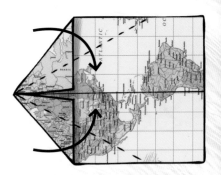

3. Fold in the two sides again, lining up the folded edges with the center crease. Flip the paper over.

4. Fold in the two sides, lining up the edges with the center crease.

5. Refold the plane in half away from you along the center crease.

6. Open up the side folds so that the "wings" lie flat on the top. Place a small piece of clear tape on top across the wings, to keep the sides together.

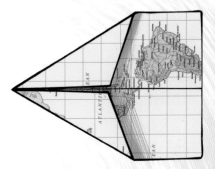

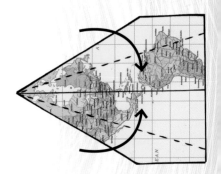

READY FOR TAKEOFF

Launch your plane by holding the bottom edge at an upward angle. Flick your wrist forward. Is your plane flying straight and far? Hook a paper clip onto the bottom near the front to add weight. Fold the back of the wings up or down. Experiment and see what happens.

TARGET PRACTICE

Invite a friend to make a plane with you. Place an object such as a hula hoop, bucket, or bowl on the floor as your target. Compete to see whose plane can reach the target first.

Make sure the folds on both sides of the plane are even with each other.

17

Secret Spy Message

Shhh! Can you keep a secret? Write down your important information, and then fold it up in a hard-to-unlock note to keep nosy people out.

Materials
1 piece of copy paper
Markers
Stickers

Steps
1. Write out your message on the piece of paper.
2. Fold it in half lengthwise, and then in half again so you have a long strip.
3. Fold one end upward in the center of the strip.

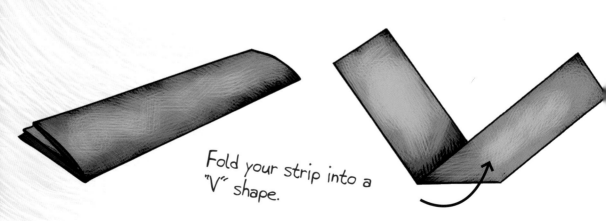

Fold your strip into a "V" shape.

4. Fold the same end back and behind so it points out the bottom.
5. Fold the end of the strip upward. Tuck it into the triangle shape.
6. Fold the other end back and behind.
7. Fold the end in and tuck it into the triangle.
8. Decorate your note with top-secret messages, stickers, and designs.

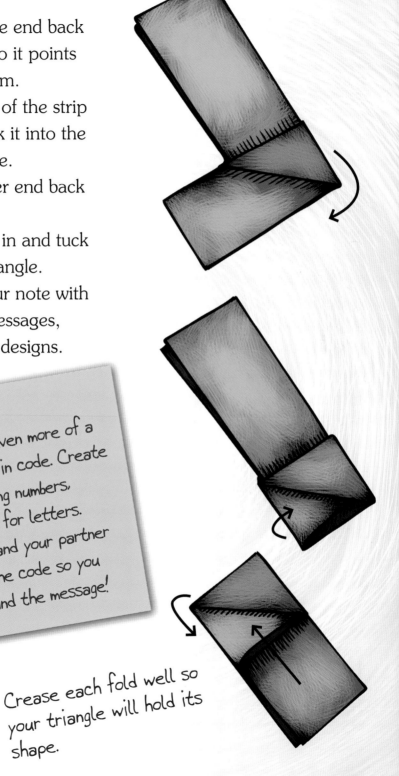

SUPER SECRET!
Make your message even more of a mystery by writing it in code. Create a code by substituting numbers, symbols, or pictures for letters. Be sure that you and your partner have the key to the code so you can both understand the message!

Crease each fold well so your triangle will hold its shape.

Gum Wrapper Gecko

You can make any shape you want using gum wrapper chains.

Gum wrapper chains are made of gum wrappers folded into links. You can make this little critter by attaching chains together. Besides gum wrappers, you can use any paper cut to size, such as magazine pages, candy wrappers, or wrapping paper. Just make sure the paper is not too thick.

Materials

3 to 4 sheets of copy paper
   (or about 40 stick gum wrappers,
   each cut in half lengthwise)
Ruler
Duct tape
Scissors and cutting mat

MAKE A PLAN

Draw out a plan on graph paper before you get started. This will help you see how many links you need, what colors to use, and how you want to arrange them. You can refer to your plan when you are working. You'll always know which link to attach next.

Steps

1. Cut out 76 1 x 2¾-inch (2.5 x 7 cm) pieces of paper.
2. Fold one piece of paper in half lengthwise. Unfold.
3. Fold each of the long edges into the center line.
4. Fold the strip in half along the center line.
5. Fold the strip in half from side to side and unfold.
6. Fold the two ends into the center. Then fold the center in half. The paper will form a small V shape. Continue with the rest of the scraps of paper until you have 76 links.
7. To start your paper chain, slip the tips of one link into the flaps of another. Pull the link all the way through.
8. Turn your work so you can slip another link into the second one.

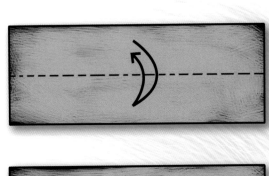

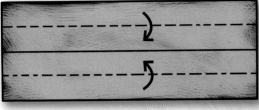

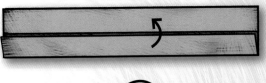

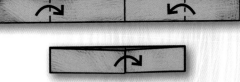

Hook each link inside of the next.

9. The chain will start forming a zigzag shape. Continue adding links until you make a chain 30 links long. This will be the center of the gecko's body.

10. Make 8 more chains as follows:

For the body:
• 2 chains 10 links long

For the head:
• 1 chain 4 links long
• 1 chain 6 links long

For the legs:
• 4 chains 4 links long

11. To attach the chains together, cut a piece of duct tape a little longer than your longest chain. Lay the tape sticky side up on a flat surface. Place the longest chain down the middle of the tape. Tuck the head and body chains next to it. Press down well.

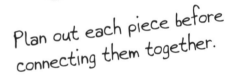

Plan out each piece before connecting them together.

12. With an adult's help, use your scissors to trim off the extra duct tape around the edges.

13. Flip your gecko over, taped side up. Lay two smaller pieces of tape, sticky side down, across his body sticking out the sides. This tape will hold on the legs.

14. Flip it back over. Lay the legs into position and press down. Trim the extra tape with the scissors. This part can be tricky, so ask an adult for help if you need it.

Tic-Tac-Toe in a Box

You can make your own board game to play on a rainy day.

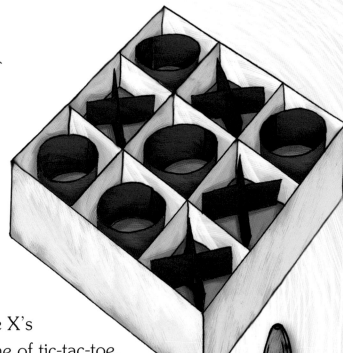

Make a box and some X's and O's to play a game of tic-tac-toe. You can also use this box to display a collection or keep small items organized on your desk or in a drawer.

Materials

10 x 10-inch (25.4 x 25.4 cm)
  mat board
Ruler
Pencil
Scissors, or craft knife and
  cutting mat

Glue
4 clips
2 colors of card stock paper
Clear tape

Steps

To Make the Box

1. Lay the mat board on your work surface, colored side up.
2. Use a ruler to measure and draw a 6-inch (15 cm) square in the center of the board. Then measure and draw a 2-inch (5 cm) frame all around it. This will make a box that is 6 inches wide on all sides and 2 inches deep.
3. Ask an adult to help you cut 2 inches into each corner using the craft knife.
4. Score all of the other lines with a ruler and scissors.
5. Fold back on the scored lines. Flip the mat board over. A box shape will start to form.
6. Squeeze glue onto the square flaps at each corner. Press them flat onto the sides of the box.
7. Hold each corner in place with a strong clip. Set the box aside to dry.
8. Use scissors or a craft knife to cut four strips of mat board, each 6 inches long and 2 inches wide.

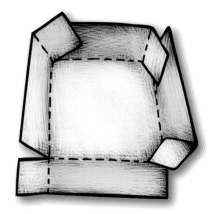

Measure your slots twice to make sure they are just right.

9. Use a ruler to measure and mark lines every 2 inches along each strip.
10. Cut slots along these lines 1 inch into the center of the strip.
11. Slide the strips into each other to make a **grid**.
12. Place the grid inside the box.

To Make the Game Pieces (5 X's and 5 O's)

1. Cut one color of card stock into ten 2 x 2¼-inch (5 x 5.7 cm) rectangles. Take two of the rectangles. Cut slots in the middle of the 2¼-inch sides. Slide the slots together. **Secure** with tape on both sides. Repeat with the rest of the rectangles (*see directions page 14*).
2. Cut the other color of card stock into five 6 x 2-inch (15 x 5 cm) strips. Roll each strip into a tube shape and secure the ends with clear tape.
3. Place your X's and O's in the box grid for a fun game of tic-tac-toe!

Make your X's and O's different colors.

Have a Ball with a Party Piñata

No party is complete without games and treats. A piñata is both! Recycle old newspapers to make a party game out of papier-mâché. Decorate it like a baseball for a sports-themed party, or be creative and use a design of your choice. You'll need to start this project five days before your party.

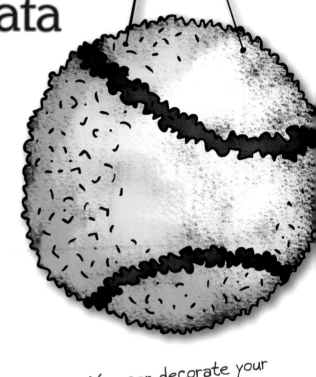

You can decorate your piñata to look like any kind of sports ball.

Materials

Flour	Plastic container	Pencil
Water	Scissors	Red and white
Bowl	String	tissue paper
Whisk	Masking tape	White glue
Newspaper	Small candies	
Balloon	Confetti	

Spread a towel or old newspapers under your work area to avoid making a mess.

Steps

1. Mix one part flour with two parts water in the bowl with a whisk. This paste mixture should be thick and not too runny.
2. Blow up a balloon and knot the end. Set it in the container so it won't roll around.
3. Tear newspaper into 1-inch (2.5 cm) strips. Dip a strip into the paste. Run your fingers down the strip over the bowl to wipe off the **excess** paste. Lay it on the balloon and press flat.
4. Repeat, laying the next strip slightly overlapping the first. Continue dipping and laying strips until the entire balloon is covered.
5. Set the balloon in the container and let it dry overnight. Repeat the **process** the next day, and again the next so that you have three layers of paper in all.

Wait until the paper is dry before cutting it.

6. On the fourth day, when the paper is dry, you can fill and decorate your piñata. Cut a flap on the end of the balloon. This will pop the balloon. Pull it out of the piñata.

7. Reach in and poke a hole with the scissors about halfway down the piñata on each side. Thread the string through the holes and tie the ends together. Tape the string up the sides of the piñata so it lies flat.

8. Pour in your candy and confetti. Tape the flap closed.

9. Draw lines on your piñata for the seams of the baseball. Cut the red tissue paper into small squares and crumple them. Glue them to the piñata along the lines.

10. Cut and crumple the white tissue paper. Fill in the rest of the surface with the white tufts of tissue. Be sure to cover the tape, strings, and flap. Let your piñata dry for a few hours.

At party time, hang your piñata, and use a baseball bat to break it and knock out all the goodies. Be sure you have plenty of room to swing safely!

EASY CLEANUP
Because the paste is just made of flour and water, you can clean up your hands, the bowl and your workspace with soap and warm water. If you can, clean up while the paste is still wet. Dry paste will harden and be harder to scrape off.

Rethink Paper

Paper is not just a surface for drawing or painting. You can turn paper into art and toys to keep you and your friends busy all day long.

How will you use paper to make a new toy or game? Invite a friend over and brainstorm some ideas. Make a project together. Then you can play with your creation when you're done. Build a pair of dice or design a set of playing cards. Fold paper into interesting creatures and make up a story with them. Create balls to toss, planes to fly, and decorations to hang.

Your creations can be small and delicate. You can construct sturdy structures, too. All you need is a blank piece of paper and your creative ideas.

Experiment with heavier and lighter paper to perfect your airplane designs.

Glossary

creases (KREES-ez) the lines of folds

excess (EK-ses) extra

grid (GRID) a pattern of crossed parallel lines

medium (MEE-dee-uhm) a material used to create art

process (PRAH-ses) the steps needed to complete a task

score (SKOR) to make an indented line in paper

secure (si-KYOOR) to hold together

tablets (TAB-lits) flat pieces of stone

textures (TEKS-churz) the way things feel

three-dimensional (THREE dih-MEN-shun-uhl) having height, width, and depth

transform (trans-FORM) to change

For More Information

Books

Gonzales, Ben A. *Paper, Scissors, Sculpt! Creating Cut-and-Fold Animals.* New York: Sterling Publishing Company, 2005.

Jackson, Paul. *Origami Toys That Tumble, Fly, and Spin.* Layton, Utah: Gibbs Smith, 2010.

Rhatigan, Joe. *Paper Fantastic: 50 Creative Projects to Fold, Cut, Glue, Paint & Weave.* New York: Lark Books, 2004.

Wickings, Ruth. *Pop-Up: Everything You Need to Create Your Own Pop-Up Book.* Somerville, MA: Candlewick Press, 2010.

Web Sites

Art Projects for Kids

www.artprojectsforkids.org/

Check out some new ideas for paper projects.

Exploratorium Magazine Online: Exploring Origami

www.exploratorium.edu/exploring/paper/index.html

Learn more about the ancient art of origami.

National Wildlife Federation: Fun Paper Recycling Projects

www.nwf.org/Global-Warming/Personal-Solutions/ Reduce-Reuse-Recycle/Paper/Fun-Paper-Projects.aspx

Get some ideas for projects made out of reused paper.

Index

About the Author

Dana Meachen Rau is the author of more than 300 books for children on many topics, including science, history, cooking, and crafts. She creates, experiments, researches, and writes from her home office in Burlington, Connecticut.